W9-CLY-681

SPACE
CRUSADERS

# Scott Kelly

## Remarkable Space Resident

Jessie Alkire

Checkerboard
Library

An Imprint of Abdo Publishing
abdobooks.com

# ABDOBOOKS.COM

Published by Abdo Publishing, a division of ABDO, PO Box 398166, Minneapolis, Minnesota 55439.
Copyright © 2019 by Abdo Consulting Group, Inc. International copyrights reserved in all countries.
No part of this book may be reproduced in any form without written permission from the publisher.
Checkerboard Library™ is a trademark and logo of Abdo Publishing.

Printed in the United States of America, North Mankato, Minnesota
102018
012019

 THIS BOOK CONTAINS
RECYCLED MATERIALS

Design: Kelly Doudna, Mighty Media, Inc.
Production: Mighty Media, Inc.
Editor: Liz Salzmann
Front Cover Photographs: NASA (both)
Back Cover Photographs: NASA (Aldrin, ISS, space shuttle, Apollo rocket), Shutterstock (planets)
Interior Photographs: Alamy, p. 13; Evan Agostini/Invision/AP, p. 21; Jrc1234 at English Wikipedia, p. 28 (top right); NASA,
pp. 5, 8, 9, 17, 19, 23 (top left, top right, bottom left, bottom center, bottom right); NASA, 25, 27, 29 (top left, top right, bottom);
NASA Johnson/Flickr, pp. 7, 28 (top left); NASA/Robert Markowitz, pp. 15, 28 (bottom); Victor Chu Photography, care of
SUNY Maritime College, p. 11

Library of Congress Control Number: 2018948528

**Publisher's Cataloging-in-Publication Data**
Names: Alkire, Jessie, author.
Title: Scott Kelly: remarkable space resident / by Jessie Alkire.
Other title: Remarkable space resident
Description: Minneapolis, Minnesota : Abdo Publishing, 2019 | Series: Space
    crusaders | Includes online resources and index.
Identifiers: ISBN 9781532117022 (lib. bdg.) | ISBN 9781532159862 (ebook)
Subjects: LCSH: Kelly, Scott, 1964- --Juvenile literature. | Astronauts--United
    States--Biography--Juvenile literature. | Space travelers--Biography--Juvenile
    literature. | ISS (International Space Station)--Juvenile literature.
Classification: DDC 629.450 [B]--dc23

# Contents

# 1 Space Life

Scott Kelly is an American astronaut. He is best known for living aboard the International Space Station for a year. He was the first American to stay in space that long. Before joining **NASA**, Kelly also served in the US Navy.

Before Kelly was an astronaut, he struggled in school. He could never focus in the classroom. However, once he realized he wanted to be an astronaut, Kelly was determined to achieve his goals. And he never gave up!

Kelly worked at NASA for 20 years. During this time, he went on four missions to space. He spent a total of 520 days in space. While on his yearlong mission, Kelly **participated** in NASA's **Twins** Study with his twin brother, Mark. The study examines how the human body is affected by long-term space residency. This study could help determine whether humans can travel to and live on other planets, such as Mars!

# 2 Challenging Childhood

Scott Kelly was born on February 21, 1964, in Orange, New Jersey. Scott was born just after his **twin** brother, Mark. Their parents were Patricia and Richard Kelly.

Scott's early life was turbulent. Richard was an **alcoholic**. He sometimes left the family alone for days at a time. As a result, Scott and Mark spent much of their time with their grandparents. Scott enjoyed the stability and comfort of his grandparents' home.

Scott and Mark were both energetic children who loved to take risks. They often rode their bikes and fished together. The brothers sometimes got hurt doing **stunts** or accepting risky dares.

When Scott was 11 years old, his mother decided to become a police officer. She studied and trained hard. The physical fitness exam was especially difficult for Patricia because she was a small woman. But her hard work paid off and she passed the exam. Scott looked up to his mother for achieving her goals and never giving up.

Scott (*left*) and Mark often wore matching outfits when they were young.

As a teenager, Scott didn't enjoy school. He was bored and restless in his classes. However, Scott found something he could focus on and enjoy outside of school. He became a volunteer emergency medical technician (EMT). Scott enjoyed the training and could stay focused, something he never experienced in school.

Scott worked his way from a volunteer EMT to a paid position. He loved the excitement of his work as an EMT. Scott decided to study to become a doctor.

Scott graduated from Mountain High School in 1982. That fall, he started college at the University of Maryland. However, Scott faced the same difficulties in college that he had in high school. He couldn't focus and often didn't go to class at all.

Everything changed when Scott read *The Right Stuff* by Tom Wolfe. The book was about pilots and astronauts. Scott knew he had found his calling. He would become a pilot and astronaut! He was finally excited about his future.

In 1962, John Glenn became the first US astronaut to orbit Earth.

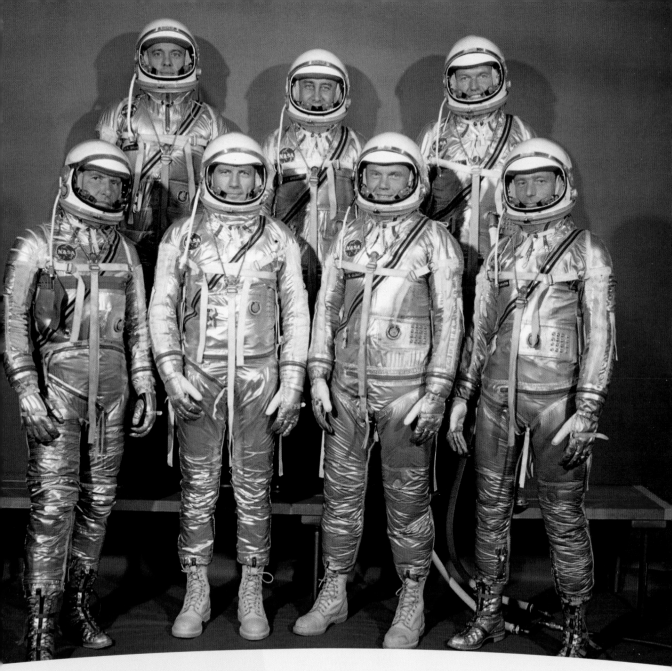

*The Right Stuff* was about the first seven astronauts selected by NASA in 1959. These astronauts included (*left to right*) Walter Schirra, Donald Slayton, John Glenn, M. Scott Carpenter, Alan Shepard, Virgil Grissom, and L. Gordon Cooper.

# 3 New Beginnings

Kelly realized that he would have to study harder to reach his goal of becoming an astronaut. The first step was being accepted to a military school. To do this, Kelly needed to take advanced classes and get good grades at the University of Maryland. So, in spring 1983, he took a **calculus** class.

Every night, Kelly studied the problems in his calculus textbook. He noticed his understanding of the material was improving each day. Kelly earned a B-minus in the class. He considered it one of his greatest achievements. It proved he could study and learn something difficult.

Kelly worked to improve his work in other classes at Maryland as well. He did well enough to be accepted at the State University of New York (SUNY) Maritime College. This college focused on military preparation. In 1983, Kelly transferred to SUNY Maritime and did extremely well. On one of his first exams, Kelly received a perfect score. This was a turning point in Kelly's relationship with school. From then on, he enjoyed it.

**STELLAR!**
SUNY Maritime was founded in 1874. It is the longest-running nautical school in the United States.

Kelly visited SUNY Maritime in May 2016.  He met with current students and spoke at the college's Admiral's Scholarship Dinner.

While at SUNY, Kelly joined the Reserve Officers' Training Corps (ROTC).  He received a full **scholarship** from ROTC after his first **semester**.  Throughout college, Kelly and his ROTC unit went on trips at sea to prepare for joining the US Navy.

# 4 The US Navy

Kelly graduated from SUNY Maritime in 1987. Kelly then joined the US Navy. In the navy, he attended flight school in Pensacola, Florida.

In flight school, Kelly learned about aircraft design, **aviation**, navigation, and more. In addition to classes, Kelly underwent weeks of fitness and swimming training. Like all branches of the military, the navy requires their members to be physically fit. And swimming skills are important in the navy because many navy assignments are on the water.

After Kelly passed the classroom and physical training, it was time to fly aircraft. Kelly was trained to fly the T-34C Turbo Mentor. Kelly passed his training in 1988. He was then assigned to a jet **squadron** at the Naval Air Station in Beeville, Texas.

About a year later, Kelly was assigned to a squadron in Virginia Beach, Virginia. There, he learned to fly the F-14 Tomcat. Kelly spent the next few years going on missions for the US Navy.

While stationed in Virginia Beach, Kelly met Leslie Yandell. The two began dating. In 1992, they got married. Shortly after,

The T–34C Turbo Mentor was the primary airplane used to train US Navy pilots from the 1970s to 2009.

Kelly was accepted to the United States Naval Test Pilot School in Patuxent River, Maryland. In 1994, Kelly graduated from test pilot school. He joined a **squadron** that flew and tested advanced fighter jets.

# 5 Space Dreams

As Kelly's career was advancing, his family was growing. In 1994, the Kellys had a baby girl, Samantha. Kelly also began thinking more about his dreams of becoming an astronaut.

Kelly decided to apply to **NASA** in 1995. He assumed he would be rejected because many people don't make it the first time. But he was accepted! NASA also accepted Kelly's brother, Mark, who had applied at the same time.

In 1996, Kelly and his family moved to Houston, Texas, so Kelly could begin NASA training. The biggest part of Kelly's training was studying space shuttles. He learned every detail about space shuttle parts and how they worked. Kelly practiced all the operations of a space shuttle until he could perform them perfectly. He also learned about geology, **meteorology**, **physics**, and more.

## STELLAR!

There are more than a million parts that make up a space shuttle. And there are two thousand switches and circuit breakers in the cockpit.

Mark (*left*) and Scott Kelly are the first twin astronauts.

# 6 First Mission

In 1999, Kelly was assigned to his first **NASA** mission. The mission was called STS-103. Kelly would be part of a crew going into space on the space shuttle *Discovery*. He was assigned to pilot the spacecraft. The crew would repair the Hubble Space Telescope.

Kelly and the rest of the crew spent several months training for the mission. Their mission was delayed several times but finally launched on December 19. After launching, it took two days for *Discovery* to reach the Hubble Space Telescope.

On the third day, crew members Steve Smith and John Grunsfeld went on their first **space walk**. They replaced three of the **gyroscopes** on the Hubble. The Hubble has six gyroscopes that help it navigate. Two more space walks occurred in the following days to replace other equipment on the telescope.

The crew returned to Earth on December 27. After his first flight, Kelly wondered what was next for his career. He soon received an answer. In 2000, Kelly

## STELLAR!

The Hubble Space Telescope has been orbiting Earth since 1990. It photographs planets, stars, and **galaxies**. The telescope is as long as a school bus!

As the STS-103 pilot, Kelly would go over checklists on *Discovery*'s flight deck to make sure procedures were followed correctly.

accepted an offer from **NASA** to be its director of operations in Russia. In this job, Kelly worked with Russia's space agency. He also helped develop training plans to teach international crews to work together.

# 7 Return to Space

After a year working in Russia, Kelly returned to the United States. He was assigned to be commander of a space shuttle mission, STS-118. The mission was planned for October 2003. However, it was postponed after the explosion of the *Columbia* space shuttle in February 2003.

In 1981, the *Columbia* had become the first US space shuttle to orbit Earth. It had been used on 27 additional space missions since then. However, on its twenty-eighth mission, an accident created a hole in one wing of the shuttle. In order to reenter Earth's atmosphere, the shuttle had to pass through an area of extreme heat. The hole in the wing allowed this heat to enter the shuttle, causing it to explode.

Before launching another space shuttle, the scientists at **NASA** needed to make sure such an accident wouldn't happen again. Although Kelly's second mission was postponed, he and his crew continued to prepare for it. There were also new developments in Kelly's family life. In 2003, Kelly's second daughter, Charlotte, was born.

The seven astronauts who died in the *Columbia* explosion were (*left to right*) David Brown, Rick Husband, Laurel Clark, Kalpana Chawla, Michael Anderson, William McCool, and Ilan Ramon.

STS-118 finally launched on August 8, 2007. The purpose of the mission was to deliver supplies to the International Space Station (ISS). Since Kelly had flown before, he was able to relax more on STS-118. The mission lasted 12 days.

A few months after STS-118, Kelly was assigned to a long mission aboard the ISS. He would live on the station for six months. Kelly trained for the mission for two years.

As Kelly prepared to live in space, he experienced major changes in his personal life. He and Leslie divorced in 2009. Soon afterward, Kelly began dating Amiko Kauderer. Kauderer was a fellow **NASA** employee Kelly had known for years.

Kelly knew it would be hard to be away from Kauderer and his daughters for so long. But he was excited about traveling to the ISS. On October 7, 2010, Kelly launched into space.

In November, Kelly became commander of the ISS. He worked with many astronauts from other countries who came to the ISS. Kelly returned to Earth on March 16, 2011. His experiences on the ISS would soon help him on an even longer mission!

## STELLAR!

The ISS is a space station orbiting Earth. Space agencies in the United States, Russia, and several other nations worked together to build it. Construction began in 1998. Astronauts have been living aboard the ISS since 2000.

Kelly, Charlotte, and Kauderer attended the 2016 opening of *A Beautiful Planet*. It is a movie about Earth that was filmed in 2015 by Kelly and other ISS crew members.

# 8 A Year in Space

In 2012, the US and Russia began planning the One-Year Mission. Each country would send someone to live on the ISS for a year. This had never been done before. At that point, the longest anyone had stayed on the ISS was six months.

The idea of building a permanent settlement on Mars was becoming popular. Space agencies such as **NASA** and private companies such as SpaceX and Boeing were researching the possibilities. One major concern was what effects long-term stays in space would have on the human body and mind. The One-Year Mission would be a way to test this.

Russia chose astronaut Mikhail Kornienko for the One-Year Mission. NASA chose Kelly. One reason Kelly was chosen for this mission was that he had a **twin** brother. Mark would remain on Earth. Scientists would be able to compare his physical condition to Kelly's. This study is known as NASA's Twins Study.

On March 27, 2015, Kelly launched into space. In addition to Kornienko, astronaut Gennady Padalka also came along. But Padalka would only stay on the ISS for a few months. Each trip to the ISS is called an expedition. The flight that brought Kelly

# ISS EXPEDITION 43

### TERRY VIRTS (1967– )

+ NASA astronaut
+ Commander of Expedition 43
+ Orbited Earth more than 3,600 times in his 16-year career

### MIKHAIL "MISHA" KORNIENKO (1960– )

+ Russian astronaut
+ Served as flight engineer on ISS Expeditions 23 and 24
+ Was part of the One-Year Mission

### GENNADY PADALKA (1958– )

+ Russian astronaut
+ Served as commander of Russia's Mir space station
+ Has visited the ISS four times

### ANTON SHKAPLEROV (1972– )

+ Russian astronaut
+ Returned to the ISS on Expedition 54 in December 2017
+ Went on a space walk that lasted more than eight hours

### SAMANTHA CRISTOFORETTI (1977– )

+ Italian astronaut
+ Captain in the Italian Air Force
+ Time spent on the ISS marked the longest spaceflight for a woman

to the ISS was Expedition 43. While he was there, three more expeditions occurred. Kelly returned to Earth on Expedition 46.

Once aboard the space station, Kelly quickly became accustomed to life in space. Life on the ISS is very organized. There are specific activities for each hour of the day. These include doing experiments, eating meals, and exercising.

Exercise was especially important. If astronauts on the ISS don't exercise, their bones get weaker. This is because of the low gravity in space. In low gravity, the bones don't have to work as hard to support the body, so they get weaker. Exercise helps the bones stay strong.

Kelly and the other crew members were responsible for completing station maintenance and conducting experiments. Many of these experiments were about gravity and health. Kelly worked mostly on experiments about the health effects of living in space. He logged the food he ate, took blood samples, and gathered other data on his physical condition.

Over the course of the yearlong mission, Kelly and his fellow crew members completed 400 experiments. They also developed strong friendships with one another. But by the end of the mission, Kelly was ready to return to Earth and to his family.

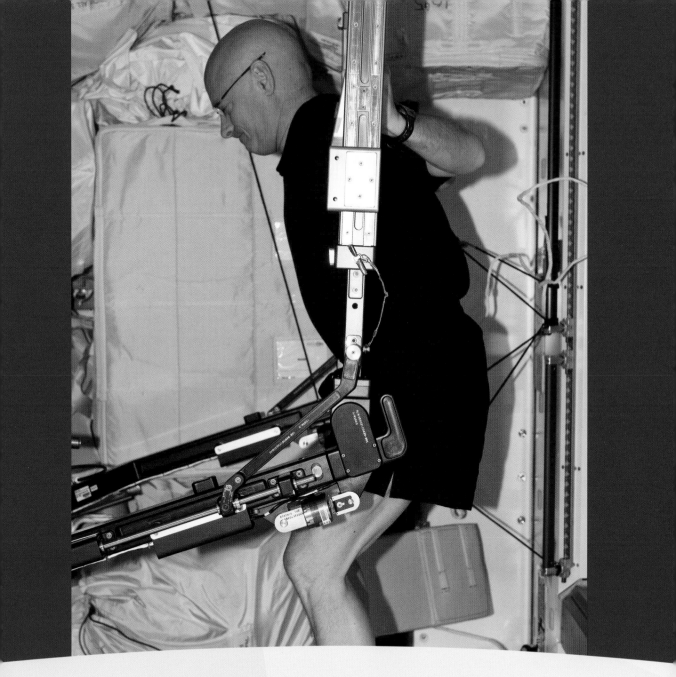

Kelly exercises aboard the ISS using a special piece of
equipment called the advanced Resistive Exercise Device.

# The Future of Space Travel

Kelly returned to Earth on March 1, 2016. He experienced health issues when he returned, including **nausea**, rashes, and swollen limbs. However, his health recovered fully after a few months.

**NASA's Twins** Study is ongoing. Kelly and his brother will be studied for many years to learn the long-term effects of Kelly's year in space. Kelly hopes this data will continue to yield new discoveries over time.

Kelly retired from NASA in April 2016. He published a **memoir**, *Endurance*, in 2017. The book discusses Kelly's life and offers an in-depth look at his yearlong ISS mission. Kelly learned much about himself, space travel, and working with others during his ISS residency.

Kelly thinks the ISS is important for learning more about space travel and conducting other scientific research. And since people from many countries work together on the ISS, it also helps promote international peace and understanding. Space remains a largely unknown frontier. But Kelly's space travels will continue to provide answers for years to come.

In June 2017, Kelly spoke at an event that opened the Kennedy Space Center's "Summer of Mars." This was an exhibit about NASA's studies of Mars.

# Timeline

Scott Kelly is born
on February 21.

## 1964

Kelly graduates from SUNY
Maritime College.  He moves to
Florida for Navy flight school.

## 1987

## 1982

Scott reads *The Right
Stuff* and decides
to become a pilot
and astronaut.

## 1996

Kelly is accepted to NASA along with his twin
brother, Mark.  He starts training in Houston, Texas.

Kelly serves as pilot for
the STS-103 mission
to fix the Hubble
Space Telescope.

**1999**

Kelly participates
in a historic
yearlong mission
aboard the
International
Space Station.

**2015**

**2007**

Kelly serves as
commander for the
STS-118 mission to
bring supplies to
the International
Space Station.

**2016**

Kelly retires from NASA.

**2017**

Kelly's memoir,
*Endurance*,
is published.

# Glossary

**alcoholic**—a person with a disorder in which he or she cannot control the urge to drink alcohol.

**aviation**—the operation and navigation of aircraft.

**calculus**—an advanced branch of math.

**galaxy**—a very large group of stars, planets, and other objects in space.

**gyroscope**—a spinning wheel in a frame that allows it to tilt in different directions.

**memoir** (MEHM-wahr)—a written account of a person's experiences.

**meteorology** (mee-tee-uh-RAH-luh-jee)—a science that deals with weather and the atmosphere.

**NASA**—National Aeronautics and Space Administration. NASA is a US government agency that manages the nation's space program and conducts flight research.

**nausea**—the feeling of being about to throw up.

**participate**—to take part or share in something.

**physics**—a science that studies matter and energy and how they interact.

**scholarship**—money or aid given to help a student continue his or her studies.

semester—half of a school year.

space walk—an activity in which an astronaut does work outside a spacecraft while it is in space.

squadron—an organized group of soldiers, ships, or aircraft.

stunt—an unusual or difficult activity.

twin—one of two children born at the same birth to the same mother.

# Index